Seasons in the South

"While the earth remains, seedtime and harvest, and cold and heat, and summer and winter, and day and night shall not cease."

Genesis 8:22

Seasons in the South

Ginny McCormack

Photography by Jarrod Cecil

Additional photography by
Noah Maier and Taylor Wright

Recipe development, food styling
and floral design by Ginny McCormack

Southern Sisters Publishing

Seasons in the South

Website: www.GinnyMcCormackCooks.com
Email: contactginnymccormack@gmail.com

Recipe development, food styling and floral design by Ginny McCormack

Photography by Jarrod Cecil, Noah Maier, Taylor Wright
www.jarrodbcecil.com
www.taylorwrightphotography.com

Layout by Smartegies LLC

Published in the United States by Southern Sisters Publishing

ISBN 978-0-692-30081-7

Printed in China by TSE Worldwide Press Inc.
www.tseworldwidepress.com

 For my dearest blessings, my children,
Rebecca, Jack, Catherine and Kelly

"If I ever move away from the South, I think the one thing I would miss the most would be cornbread. Definitely. Cornbread. And sweet tea. I cannot imagine a day without good sweet tea. And homemade peach jam. If I moved away from the South I could ask my friends to send me some peach jam but it would not be the same without good biscuits to put it on, so I would miss those too. Surely I would also miss fried green tomatoes. And catfish. And real chopped pork barbecue - the kind we make in the South and serve with white bread for dipping in the sauce. I would also miss sweet potato casserole. And collard greens. And Lord, how I would miss pimento cheese. Oh, I forgot about banana pudding. On second thought, that may be the one thing I would miss the most if I ever moved away from the South."

Sarah Livingston, Beaufort, SC

Come away with me and enjoy the beauty and flavors of the southern seasons! When asked which one is my favorite, I claim a woman's prerogative to change her mind. And I always do. For me, my favorite season is the one that is just around the corner. This is because anticipation is an essential requisite for true enjoyment of any season. Here in the South we bask in the warmer seasons in ways most befitting the southern lifestyle, yet as the heat fades away we welcome the cool relief of autumn with the greatest enthusiasm. Despite my decades of experience living through the seasons, I am always surprised by the beauty of a harvest moon on a fall evening or a spontaneous eruption of daffodils from the earth in spring. Deep down I know they're coming, yet they always feel like unexpected gifts when they finally arrive.

Ginny McCormack

Spring

Summer

Autumn

Winter

SPRING

"It's spring fever. That is what the name of it is. And when you've got it, you want — oh, you don't quite know what it is you do want, but it just fairly makes your heart ache, you want it so!"

Mark Twain, American author and humorist

Springtime Dinner in the Garden

The Menu

Pineapple and Hickory Bacon Cheese Log

Southern Fruited Chicken Salad

Bibb and Radish Salad with White Balsamic Vinaigrette

Toasted Baguette Slices

Carrot Cupcakes with Cream Cheese Frosting

"I like a cook who smiles out loud when she tastes her own work. Let God worry about her modesty; I want to see her enthusiasm."

Robert Farrar Capon, American priest, author and food columnist

Ah, springtime. Is there a more fitting reward in the entire world for enduring the cold confinement of winter? Just when we think the cold weather will not end, Mother Nature sends us those ever-so-welcome glimmers of springtime. The signs are subtle at first, as the sun begins warming the earth and tiny green buds become visible on the tips of the tree branches. Before long the daffodils and tulips force their way up through the ground and stretch themselves toward heaven as the world around them begins to warm and come alive with color. Yes, indeed. Spring arrives and treats us all to its magnificent glory. So what to do? Well, here in the South we dine outdoors, of course. The sights and scents of the season often compel us to set a table beneath the trees – or a blanket on the grass – and enjoy our meal while noting how delicious the food tastes when eaten outdoors. This classic southern experience is both delightful and worthy of repeating as often as possible.

"There is something civilized about a cloth napkin. It lends the proper sense of attitude to a meal that a paper towel, despite its best effort, cannot muster."

Cora Pate Mulford, Marietta, GA

17

Pineapple and Hickory Bacon Cheese Log

Fruit and cheese always pair beautifully together. Add bacon and you've got a match made in heaven.

8 oz. cream cheese, slightly softened

8 oz. white cheddar cheese, shredded

1 cup crushed pineapple, well drained

½ cup onion, finely chopped

1 tsp. garlic salt

6 slices bacon, fried crisp and crumbled

In a large bowl, combine the cheeses, pineapple, onion and garlic salt. Form the mixture into a log and roll in the crumbled bacon to cover all sides. Wrap in plastic wrap and chill until firm. Serve with crackers.

Makes 12 servings

"Bacon is the candy of meat."

Kevin Taggart, author

Chicken Salad 101

I am convinced that when chicken is mixed with mayonnaise, fruit, nuts and herbs, the result is absolute southern bliss. Chicken salad is a masterful combination of flavors and textures: savory, tender chunks of chicken, creamy mayonnaise, sweet fruit, and crunchy nuts, all enhanced with a sprinkling of salt, pepper and herbs like tarragon (my hands down favorite). A quintessentially southern dish, chicken salad is an ever welcome guest at most tables where ladies "lunch." No celebratory gathering is quite complete without it. It's as delicious on fine china at a formal ladies' luncheon as it is when nibbled directly from the bowl while standing in front of the refrigerator for a late night snack (yes, I've done that.) I love the flavor of a chicken cooked slowly in a pot with onion and celery, however, if you are short on time, pick up a perfectly good rotisserie chicken from the store and make no apologies. A good cook is, after all, always versatile.

"Aside from a glass of wine, a new pair of shoes or a kiss from the man I love, there is little else that lifts my spirit as much as a heaping serving of chicken salad — the southern version, of course."

Virginia Beaumont, Thibadeaux, LA

Southern Fruited Chicken Salad

Nearly any chopped fruit can be mixed into chicken salad with a good result. Apples, berries and dried cranberries are great additions. Tarragon adds a wonderful anise-like flavor, making it my go-to herb for chicken salad.

2 cups chicken, cooked and cut up

½ cup red seedless grapes, halved

½ cup mandarin orange segments

½ cup celery, thinly sliced

½ red onion, finely chopped

½ cup pecans, chopped

¾ cup good quality mayonnaise

1 Tbsp. lemon juice

1 Tbsp. dried tarragon

1 tsp. salt

½ tsp. pepper

In a large bowl, toss together the chicken, grapes, oranges, celery, onion and pecans. Set aside. In a small bowl, combine the mayonnaise, lemon juice, tarragon, salt and pepper. Pour the mayonnaise mixture over the chicken and toss lightly. Place in the refrigerator until chilled.

Makes 4-6 servings

Lettuce:
A Most Amiable Partner

Take a moment to contemplate lettuce. Though each American consumes nearly 30 pounds of it a year, it is rarely eaten alone as one would eat, say, an apple. Yet why do we love it so? Perhaps its appeal is in its neutrality (and its cool crunch). It could be called the Switzerland of vegetables. It is an unbiased partner with whom food can interact, and it complements the personalities of the ingredients we toss, wrap, layer or drizzle it with. Nonetheless, we may be doing this delicate leafy green a disservice if we fail to recognize the uniqueness of its many varieties. Are you in an iceberg rut? Bet you know a man who is. Try shaking things up by exploring some other varieties such as Boston (mild and sweet), Arugula (peppery), Radicchio (slightly bitter), Watercress (tender and peppery), Romaine (crisp, mild and slightly bitter), Red and Green Leaf (mild and slightly sweet), or Oak Leaf (light and sweet). Your BLT will thank you.

"When you plant lettuce, if it does not grow well, you don't blame the lettuce. You look for reasons it is not doing well. It may need fertilizer, or more water, or less sun. You never blame the lettuce. Yet if we have problems with our friends or family, we blame the other person. But if we know how to take care of them, they will grow well, like the lettuce. That is my experience."

Thich Nhat Hanh
Vietnamese teacher, author, poet

Bibb and Radish Salad
with White Balsamic Vinaigrette

It's hard to beat the simplicity of this fresh Bibb lettuce salad. White balsamic vinegar is less heavy and syrupy than traditional balsamic and won't darken the salad, making this vinaigrette a light yet flavorful alternative.

3 large heads Bibb lettuce, torn into bite size pieces

8 radishes, thinly sliced

1 medium cucumber, thinly sliced

In a large bowl, toss the lettuce with the radishes and cucumber. Just before serving, drizzle with enough dressing to coat the salad. Toss and serve.

Makes 6 servings

White Balsamic Vinaigrette

¼ cup white balsamic vinegar

1 Tbsp. lemon juice

¾ cup extra virgin olive oil

1 Tbsp. honey

½ tsp. salt

¼ tsp. pepper

In a small bowl, whisk together the vinegar and lemon juice. Slowly add the oil in a steady stream, whisking continuously. Add the honey, salt and pepper and continue whisking until smooth. Can be stored in an airtight container up to 1 week in the refrigerator.

Makes 1 cup

Toasted Baguettes Slices

These are a nice alternative to crackers when serving chicken salad. I also use them with sliced cheeses, smoked salmon and for bruschetta.

1 large or 2 medium fresh baguettes

¼ cup extra virgin olive oil

kosher salt

black pepper

2 Tbsp. fresh Italian parsley, chopped

Preheat oven to 400 degrees. Slice the baguette diagonally into ½" pieces. Place the slices on a baking sheet and brush each slice with olive oil. Sprinkle with salt and pepper. Bake the baguette slices for 15-20 minutes, turning once during baking until crisp and golden brown. Sprinkle the slices with parsley and serve. Delicious warm or room temperature.

Makes 10-12 servings

Life's meant to be sweet. Grab a cupcake and enjoy the ride.

Kimmie Easley, author, *Souls Set Free*

Carrot Cupcakes with Cream Cheese Frosting

1 cup flour

¾ cup sugar

1 tsp. ground cinnamon

1 tsp. baking soda

½ tsp. baking powder

¼ tsp. salt

⅔ cup vegetable or canola oil

2 eggs, beaten

1 ½ cups grated carrots (plus 1-2 Tbsp. for garnish)

Preheat the oven to 350 degrees. Line a 12-cup cupcake pan with liners. Combine the flour, sugar, cinnamon, baking soda, baking powder and salt in a large bowl. In a separate bowl, whisk together the oil and eggs. Add to the flour mixture and combine. Fold in the carrots and stir until incorporated. Spoon the batter into the muffin pan, filling each liner 2/3 full. Bake 13-15 minutes, or until a toothpick inserted into the center comes out clean. Cool completely before frosting.

Makes 12 cupcakes

Cream Cheese Frosting

4 oz. cream cheese, slightly softened

4 Tbsp. butter, slightly softened

1 tsp. pure vanilla extract

2 cups confectioner's sugar

In a medium bowl, blend the cream cheese, butter and vanilla. Slowly beat in the confectioner's sugar until smooth. Spread frosting on top of the cooled cupcakes and garnish with grated carrot.

Relaxing Supper on the Porch

The Menu

Low Country Crab Cakes with Remoulade Sauce

Sweet Potato Fries

Crunchy Oriental Slaw

Cornbread Muffins

Strawberry Limeade

"Just like becoming an expert in wine — you learn by drinking it, the best you can afford — you learn about great food by finding the best there is, whether simple or luxurious. Then you savor it, analyze it, discuss it with your companions, and compare it with other experiences."

Julia Child, American chef, author and television personality

"A true lady always sips her sherry while sitting on the veranda; she never gulps."

Sarabeth Devereaux, Nashville, TN

While it may be a bit of an overstatement to say that southerners invented the practice of dining on the porch, there can be little doubt (actually none at all) that we do it with impeccable style and ease. After all, our porches are natural extensions of our homes and as I always say, whatever is inside can be brought outside. And why not? How delightful it is to set a table like this one with a vintage floral tablecloth and a pitcher overflowing with alstroemeria, daisies, and hydrangeas in shades of yellow, white and fuchsia. These flowers were simply my choice on this day. On any other day I would have filled the pitcher with whatever was blooming in abundance in the garden or yard. These simple touches create such a welcoming setting for this delicious low country crab cake supper. Planning a later evening meal for company? Simply add votive candles, pour some wine and enjoy the springtime atmosphere while watching the sun set. You'll want to linger there as long as possible. I promise.

"You cannot teach a crab to walk straight."

Aristophanes, Greek playwright

Low Country Crab Cakes with Remoulade Sauce

You don't have to reside in the low country to enjoy these easy, delectable crab cakes. Though often served with tartar sauce, the remoulade sauce is a nice alternative. Try spreading the leftover sauce on sandwiches and burgers.

1 lb. fresh lump crab meat	½ tsp. salt
1 large egg	1 ¼ cups fresh bread crumbs made from
¼ cup mayonnaise	soft white bread
2 tsp. Old Bay seasoning	2 Tbsp. vegetable oil
1 tsp. Worcestershire sauce	2 Tbsp. butter

Drain the crab meat and pick through it for shells. Place it in a mixing bowl and set aside. In a small bowl, whisk together the egg, mayonnaise, Old Bay seasoning, Worcestershire sauce and salt. Add to the crab meat and mix gently until combined. Add the bread crumbs and combine gently. Do not over mix. Shape the mixture into 8 crab cakes about 1" thick. In a large skillet, heat the oil and butter over medium heat until bubbly. Cook the crab cakes for 4 minutes. Flip, reduce heat slightly, and continue cooking on the other side for 4-5 minutes until dark golden brown. Serve with *Remoulade Sauce*.

Makes 8 crab cakes

Remoulade Sauce

1 cup mayonnaise	½ cup green onions,	2 tsp. hot sauce
2 Tbsp. whole grain mustard	finely chopped	¼ tsp. black pepper
2 Tbsp. ketchup	1 stalk celery, finely chopped	Whisk together all ingredients.
1 Tbsp. lemon juice	2 cloves garlic, minced	Cover and chill 1 hour.
1 Tbsp. Worcestershire sauce	1 tsp. paprika	*Makes 2 ½ cups*

Crunchy Oriental Slaw

Sweet and tangy, this Asian salad recipe is a real crowd pleaser and perhaps my all-time favorite salad. Try it once and you'll make it again and again.

1 (16 oz.) bag shredded cole slaw or 1 lb. shredded cabbage

½ cup green onions, sliced

½ cup sliced almonds

1 pkg. Ramen noodles, crushed (Do not use the seasoning packet. Tip: crush the
    noodles inside the package with the bottom of a heavy drinking glass)

2 Tbsp. butter

Dressing:

½ cup vegetable oil

½ cup cider or white vinegar

½ cup sugar

4 Tbsp. soy sauce

Place the cole slaw and green onions in a large bowl. In a skillet, melt butter and saute almonds and noodles until golden brown. Add to the coleslaw. Combine the dressing ingredients in a saucepan and bring to boil. Cook for 2 minutes. Cool and store until ready to use. Just prior to serving, toss the dressing with the coleslaw mixture and serve immediately.

Makes 6 servings

Sweet Potato Fries

Oven baked sweet potato fries tossed with olive oil and kosher salt are a healthy and satisfying alternative to traditional French fries. Try a sprinkling of cayenne pepper for an added kick.

2 large sweet potatoes, peeled and sliced into ½" wide strips

olive oil

salt and pepper

Preheat oven to 450 degrees. Place sweet potatoes in a bowl and toss with enough olive oil to coat thoroughly. Spread the potatoes in a single layer, not touching each other, on a large baking sheet. Bake until the sweet potatoes are golden brown outside and tender inside, turning occasionally, about 20-25 minutes. Sprinkle generously with salt and pepper.

Makes 4 servings

Cornbread Muffins

This recipe freezes well so I often double it so I have an extra dozen on hand the next time I make soup or chili.

1 cup cornmeal

1 cup all-purpose flour

⅓ cup sugar

2 tsp. baking powder

½ tsp. salt

1 egg, beaten

¼ cup vegetable oil

1 cup milk

Preheat oven to 400 degrees. Line a muffin pan with paper liners. In a large bowl, combine the corn meal, flour, sugar, baking powder and salt. Add the egg, oil and milk. Mix to combine and spoon batter into the muffin cups. Bake for 15-20 minutes or until a toothpick inserted into the center comes out clean.

Makes 1 dozen

Strawberry Limeade

This 'pretty in pink' beverage looks and tastes like springtime!

3 cups fresh strawberries, quartered

2 cups lime juice

1 ½ cups sugar

10 cups cold water

ice

lime wedges for garnish, if desired

Blend the strawberries and lime juice in a blender until smooth.   Pour the mixture into a large pitcher.   Add the sugar and water and stir until sugar dissolves. Serve over ice and garnish with lime wedges.

Makes 8 servings

"I remember suppers on our front porch when I was a little girl. My sisters and I talked nonstop and my brother never got a word in edgewise. Charlie the dog would lie beside my chair. Sometimes I'd accidentally drop a morsel of food on the floor. Well, occasionally I did it on purpose. Charlie knew that, which is why he always stayed so close to me. I remember once it rained really hard during supper. The sky grew dark, thunder rumbled, the wind began to blow and the rains showered down from heaven. Charlie ran inside the house. I thought my mother would tell us all to go inside, but she didn't. We just sat there and watched the rainstorm. We felt safe together on that front porch. I remember the scent of the rain as it blew across the table on a breeze. It was all quite beautiful. I recall wishing it would rain like that every day."

Jeannette Mulford, Charleston, SC

"I am told that gratefulness is the key to happiness. I believe this is true. I am grateful for all the things God has given me, and of course I mean the big things like health and family and freedom. However, I am also extremely grateful for little things like pound cake, good books, shoe shopping, moon pies and Coca-Cola to name a few. This may explain why I am one of the happiest people I know."

Sarah Livingston, Beaufort, SC

Afternoon Dining by the Lake

The Menu

Roasted Lamb Chops with Apple Mint Chutney

Old Fashioned Cold Pea Salad

Buttered Parsley Noodles

Honey Muffins

Dark Chocolate Mousse with Raspberries

When it comes to creating mood and atmosphere for any setting, perhaps one of the greatest influences is light, yet few of us give it much consideration. There is no doubt that in the creation of this book, where so many of my concepts and ideas are expressed visually through photography, light is an essential contributor. The difference between a good and poor photo often hinges upon lighting. In much the same way, we can harness the power and beauty of light in our surroundings by the choices we make. For example, the glow from carefully placed candles can transform the mood of a room in a way not achieved by an overhead light. And if I time it just right, I can walk along the lake by my home just as the morning sun clears the tree tops and casts a shimmering light across the water that sparkles like a million crystals. All I can do is stop and stare. On this beautiful spring afternoon, the sunshine was filtering through the tree leaves and the light was dancing with the shadows all around us. What a lovely sight to behold.

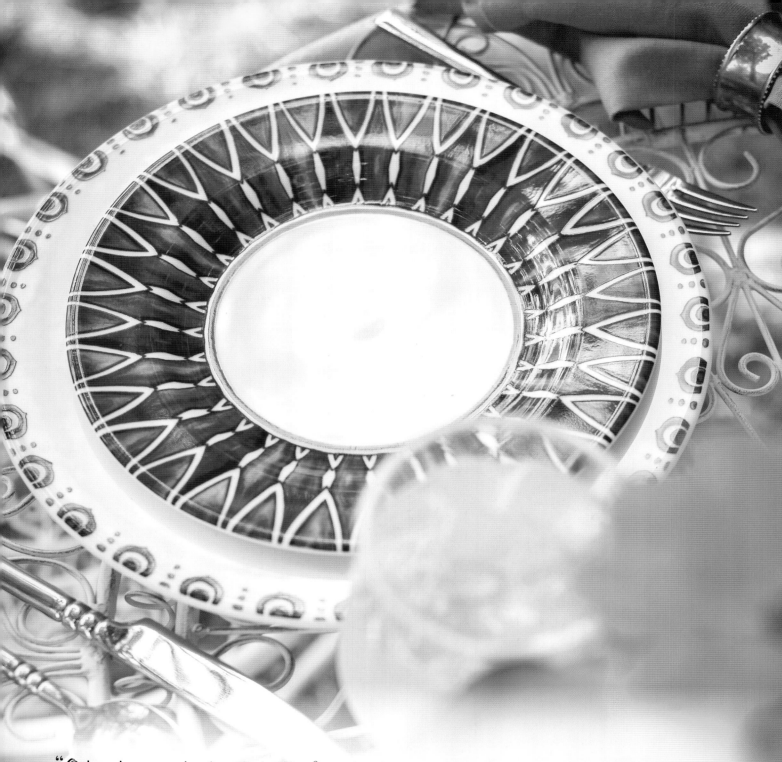

"Other than to school and church, I don't recall wearing shoes before the age of eight. I was barefoot most of the time. I fancied myself a sort of forest child, running wild outdoors. These days, I think we should encourage our children to run barefoot through the grass more often. It is a delightful part of childhood. We should encourage the adults to do the same. It helps them remember what it was like to be a child."

Hattie Montgomery, Waynesville, NC

Roasted Lamb Chops
with Apple Mint Chutney

What a treat this dish is. It's perfect for a spring menu. Although the lamb chops are the main attraction at this meal, they also make an impressive appetizer at your next soirée. The chutney is a terrific accompaniment to almost any roasted or grilled meat, especially chicken and pork.

1 ½ Tbsp. kosher salt

2 Tbsp. fresh rosemary leaves, finely chopped

4 cloves garlic, minced

½ cup Dijon mustard

1 Tbsp. balsamic vinegar

2 racks of lamb (approx. 1 lb. each)

Preheat oven to 450 degrees. In a mixing bowl, combine the salt, rosemary and garlic. Add the mustard and vinegar and whisk until fully combined. Place the lamb racks in a roasting pan with the ribs curved down. Spread the mustard mixture over the top of the lamb and let stand at room temperature for 1 hour. Roast the lamb for 25 minutes for medium-rare doneness. Remove from the oven, cover with aluminum foil and allow to rest for 15 minutes. Slice the chops into individual pieces and serve with *Apple Mint Chutney*.

Makes 4-6 servings

Apple Mint Chutney

2 Tbsp. butter

½ medium red onion, chopped

2 granny smith apples, peeled, cored and diced

⅓ cup firmly packed brown sugar

¼ cup golden raisins

3 Tbsp. apple cider vinegar

¼ tsp. salt

⅓ cup fresh mint, chopped

In a medium saucepan, melt the butter over medium heat. Add the onion and cook until soft. Stir in the apple, sugar, raisins, vinegar, salt and ⅓ cup water. Bring the mixture to a boil, then reduce heat and cook, stirring occasionally, until the mixture has thickened and the apple is tender, about 10 minutes. Remove from the heat and stir in the mint. Cool to room temperature and serve with the lamb.

Makes about 2 cups

"Give peas a chance."

Jarrod Cecil, photographer,
Seasons in the South

Old Fashioned Cold Pea Salad

I've found that even those who don't like peas often enjoy this classic salad recipe. The combination of the salty bacon and the sweetness of the peas and the creamy dressing makes this a great salad any time of year. I like to serve it during warm weather, but it also adorns many a holiday table here in the South.

2 (10 oz.) packages frozen peas, thawed and drained

6 slices bacon, cooked crisp and crumbled

1 medium red onion, chopped

3 large hard boiled eggs, peeled and chopped

¼ cup mayonnaise

¼ cup sour cream

1 Tbsp. sugar

½ tsp. salt

In a large bowl, toss together the peas, bacon, onion and eggs. In a small bowl, whisk together the mayonnaise, sour cream, sugar and salt. Pour the dressing over the pea mixture and toss gently to combine thoroughly. Cover and chill.

Makes 6-8 servings

Buttered Parsley Noodles

This was always comfort food for my kids when they were growing up. These warm, buttery egg noodles with a hint of garlic are still a favorite at my house. I love them with just about any kind of roasted meat, although you can also cover them with shredded parmesan cheese and call it a meal.

16 oz. wide egg noodles

2 chicken bouillon cubes

½ cup (1 stick) butter, cut into 8 pieces

2 cloves garlic, minced

½ cup fresh parsley, chopped

Dissolve the bouillon cubes in a large saucepan of boiling water over medium high heat. Add the egg noodles and cook according to package directions. Drain the noodles and return them to the saucepan. Add the butter and garlic to the noodles and toss until the butter is melted. Add the parsley and combine. Transfer the noodles to a serving bowl.

Makes 6-8 servings

Honey Muffins

Sweet and simple – just like life in the South.

2 cups all-purpose flour

½ cup sugar

1 Tbsp. baking powder

½ tsp. salt

1 egg

1 cup milk

¼ cup (½ stick) butter, melted

¼ cup honey

1 Tbsp. grated orange zest for garnish, if desired

Preheat oven to 400 degrees. In a large mixing bowl, combine the flour, sugar, baking powder and salt. In a separate bowl, combine the egg, milk, butter and honey. Add this to the dry mixture and stir just until incorporated.

Spoon the batter into a greased or paper-lined muffin pan until each is ¾ full. Bake for 14-17 minutes or until a toothpick inserted in the center comes out clean. Cool a few minutes before removing the muffins from the pan.

Makes 1 dozen

Dark Chocolate Mousse with Fresh Raspberries

This classic chocolate mousse is both versatile and decadently delicious. It's simple enough for everything from a girls' night in to a formal dinner party. I love rolling it up in crepes, filling a pie crust with it, or spooning it into champagne flutes for an extra fancy presentation.

8 oz. bittersweet chocolate, coarsely chopped

16 oz. heavy whipping cream, chilled

3 large egg whites

¼ cup sugar

1 pint fresh raspberries

shaved bittersweet chocolate for garnish, if desired

Place chocolate in a bowl set on top of a saucepan (a double boiler may be used) over simmering water. Stir the chocolate until melted and smooth. Remove the bowl or top of double boiler from the heat and set aside.

Using an electric mixer or stand mixer, beat the cold whipping cream until stiff. Set aside. With a mixer, beat the egg whites until they form soft peaks. Gradually add the sugar and beat until firm. With a whisk, fold the egg whites into the melted chocolate until nearly incorporated. Then fold in the whipping cream until combined. Cover and refrigerate 1 hour or until set. When ready to serve, spoon mousse into individual dishes, top with raspberries and sprinkle with shaved chocolate.

Makes 6 servings

"There is nothing better than a friend,
unless it is a friend with chocolate."

Linda Grayson, American author

SUMMER

"There's a time in each year
That we always hold dear,
Good old summer time;
With the birds and the trees-es,
And sweet scented breezes,
Good old summertime."

Lyrics by Ren Shields, *In the Good Old Summertime*

Early Summer Family Gathering

The Menu

Fully Loaded Pimento Cheese

Marinated Pork Chops with Sweet & Spicy Peach Chutney

Creamy Gruyere Cheese Grits

Charred Green Beans

Watermelon Granita

"People who love to eat are always the best people."

Julia Child, American chef, author and television personality

Of all the seasons, it is perhaps summer that is the most giving. At times it seems there is no end to its delicious bounty – and barely enough days to indulge in every wonderful fruit, vegetable and summertime delicacy that is available. A simple trip to the local farmer's market in June will confirm this. Who among us has not returned home with paper bags loaded with all manner of summer treats and wondered how we will ever eat it all before it spoils? What a delicious problem to have! On this early summer evening, the table is set with yellow flowers and festive square plates in summery shades of green to create a relaxed and colorful setting for our summer menu.

Fully Loaded Pimento Cheese

1 (8 oz.) package cream cheese, softened

4 cups sharp cheddar cheese, shredded

⅓ cup mayonnaise

1 tsp. garlic powder

1 (4 oz.) jar diced pimentos, drained

4 Tbsp. pickled jalepenos, diced

½ medium onion, finely chopped

½ cup pecans, chopped

2-3 dashes hot sauce

Preheat oven to 375 degrees. Place pecans in a single layer on a baking sheet and roast for 8-10 minutes until golden brown. Cool for 10 minutes.

In a large mixing bowl, combine the cream cheese and cheddar cheese. Add all remaining ingredients and combine thoroughly. Cover and chill for at least 1 hour.

Makes 4 cups

Marinated Pork Chops
with Sweet & Spicy Peach Chutney

This sweet and savory dish is perfect on a warm summer evening. The chutney is fabulous leftover and served with chicken, on a sandwich, or spooned over cream cheese.

⅓ cup soy sauce

⅓ cup vegetable oil

4 Tbsp. brown sugar

2 tsp. ground ginger

½ tsp. black pepper

4 bone-in pork chops, about ¾" thick

4 Tbsp. oil for cooking

In a small mixing bowl, combine the first five ingredients. Set aside 4 Tbsp. of the marinade. Place the pork chops in a gallon-size plastic bag, pour the remaining marinade over the chops and seal the bag tightly. Refrigerate for at least 45 minutes, turning the bag once halfway through.

Heat the remaining oil in a large skillet over medium high heat. Remove the pork chops from the bag and place in the skillet. Sear for 4 minutes, reduce heat to medium, flip chops and continue cooking 3-4 minutes longer. Remove the chops to a serving plate and allow to rest for at least 5 minutes. Add the reserved marinade to the skillet and cook for about a minute until slightly thickened. Spoon over the pork chops. Serve with *Sweet & Spicy Peach Chutney*.

Sweet & Spicy Peach Chutney

½ cup cider vinegar

½ cup sugar

½ cup brown sugar, packed

1 large red bell pepper, diced

1 medium onion, finely chopped

1 small jalapeno pepper, seeded and diced

⅓ cup golden raisins

2 cloves garlic, minced

1 Tbsp. fresh ginger, grated

½ tsp. salt

1 ½ lbs. fresh peaches, peeled, pits removed and coarsely chopped (one 29-oz. can sliced peaches, chopped, can be substituted)

In a saucepan over medium-high heat, place the vinegar, sugar and brown sugar. Bring to a boil. Add the red pepper, onion, jalapeno, raisins, garlic, ginger and salt. Simmer for 10 minutes. Add the peaches and simmer for an additional 10 minutes until peaches are tender. Remove from the heat and allow to cool. Serve at room temperature. Can be refrigerated for up to one week.

Makes 2 ½ cups

Gruyere Cheese Grits

It is likely that folks who claim they don't like grits have never actually tried real, stone ground, southern cheese grits, which bear no resemblance to the watery, flavorless version that comes in an envelope. Anyone who tries a true southern grits recipe like this one will no doubt feel compelled to make a public declaration of its creamy, yummy, deliciousness.

1 cup stone ground white grits

2 cups chicken broth or stock

2 cups half-n-half

1 ½ cups Gruyere cheese, shredded

kosher salt

black pepper

In a large saucepan, bring the chicken stock and half-n-half to a boil over high heat. Whisk in the grits and reduce heat to low. Cook, stirring frequently, until grits are thick and creamy, about 45 minutes. If the grits become too thick, add a little chicken stock or half-n-half. Remove grits from the heat and stir in the cheese until melted. Season to taste with salt and pepper.

Makes 4-6 servings

"There is absolutely no substitute for the best. Good food cannot be made of inferior ingredients masked with high flavor. It is true thrift to use the best ingredients available and to waste nothing."

James Beard, American author, instructor and champion of American cuisine

Charred Green Beans

This couldn't be a simpler recipe - and a most flavorful way to enjoy this classic southern green vegetable. Pan sautéing green beans in hot oil at a high temperature brings out their deliciously dark, nutty, earthy flavor. After a sprinkling of salt, you'll devour them like French fries.

1 lb. fresh green beans, washed, ends trimmed, cut into 2-inch pieces

4 Tbsp. oil

kosher salt

black pepper

Heat oil in a large sauté pan over medium high heat. Add the green beans and toss with a spoon to coat the green beans with the oil. Cook, stirring regularly, until the green beans are tender and moderately charred, 10-12 minutes or until the desired degree of doneness is achieved.

Makes 6 servings

Watermelon Granita

This frosty, sweet, fruity granita is everything a summer treat should be.

8 cups fresh, seedless watermelon, cut into chunks

Juice of 2 limes

¼ cup sugar

Place 4 cups watermelon chunks, juice of one lime and half the sugar in a blender and process until smooth. Pour the mixture into a 9 x 13 baking pan. Repeat with the remaining watermelon, lime juice and sugar and add to the baking dish. Place in the freezer for 2-3 hours then  remove and scrape the top, frozen layer to loosen it. Return to the freezer and repeat the process every two hours until the entire pan has been shaved. Cover and store in the freezer until ready to serve. Serve in pretty glasses with a wedge of fresh watermelon.

Makes 8 servings

Casual Evening at the Beach House

The Menu

Crudités with Buttermilk Herb Dressing

Bacon & Pimento Cheese Burgers on Toasted Buns

Homemade Potato Chips

Roasted Corn Salad with Avocado

Georgia Peach Cobbler

"Pull up a chair. Take a taste. Come join us. Life is so endlessly delicious."

Ruth Reichl, American food writer

Life in the South is so rich and full of delightful pleasures. Down here we can dress up a table like no one else when it comes to formal entertaining. Additionally, there is a certain appeal and elegance to the way southerners "do casual." Burlap and sterling? Of course. Wildflowers stuffed into grandma's lead crystal pitcher? You bet. We own this style and it becomes us. Try searching your cabinets, closets and attic for fun and unique pieces that can lend charm to your casual dinner table. In this case, an old beat up farm table laden with cloth linens and a heaping spray of white alstromeira creates a lovely and relaxed setting for our casual burger dinner on the porch.

Crudités with Buttermilk Herb Dressing

Assorted sliced, raw vegetables: carrots, celery, red pepper, cucumbers, green onions, radishes.

½ cup buttermilk

⅓ cup mayonnaise

2 Tbsp. olive oil

1 Tbsp. cider vinegar

1 Tbsp. parsley, chopped

1 Tbsp. thyme, chopped

1 Tbsp. chives, chopped

2 cloves garlic, minced

½ tsp. salt

¼ tsp. pepper

In a small bowl, whisk together the buttermilk, mayonnaise and olive oil until smooth. Whisk in the remaining ingredients. Serve with the crudités. Store remaining dressing in an airtight container in the refrigerator up to 1 week.

Makes about 1 cup

Bacon and Pimento Cheese Burgers

If bacon makes everything better, then imagine how delicious a burger with both bacon and pimento cheese can be. To ensure your burger is nice and moist, don't overwork the meat when forming it into loose patties and don't press down with the spatula when cooking. The juiciest and most flavorful burger is made with ground beef that is no more than 80% lean. The inevitable truth is that when it comes to burgers, the flavor is in the fat.

1 ½ lbs. ground chuck (80% lean)	green leaf lettuce
kosher salt	4 large hamburger buns or bakery rolls
pepper	1 cup *Fully Loaded Pimento Cheese*
2 Tbsp. vegetable oil	(recipe on p. 63), pecans omitted
8 slices bacon, cooked crisp and cut in half	

To toast the rolls, split them in half and place, cut side up, on a baking sheet. Bake them under a preheated broiler for about 1 minute. Watch carefully so they don't burn. Set aside.

Form meat into 4 loosely packed patties. Using your thumb, press each patty to form a depression in the center. Generously sprinkle both sides with salt and pepper.

Heat the oil in a cast iron skillet over high heat. Cook the burgers on one side for 3 minutes until slightly charred. Flip them and continue cooking for 3-4 minutes for medium-rare.

Place a large piece of green leaf lettuce on the bottom half of each roll. Next, place the burgers, 4 half-pieces of bacon and a ¼ cup scoop of Fully Loaded Pimento Cheese. Top with the toasted roll and serve.

Makes 4 servings

"My advice to young men? Marry a woman who appreciates a good burger and isn't afraid to show it. Now that's a good sign for a long and happy marriage. Nothing wrong with salads, of course, but sometimes a girl just needs to sink her teeth into some beef. Take my wife, for example. We had been dating only a short time when I took her out for a cheeseburger at a diner in my old hometown. To my surprise, she polished off that burger with great enthusiasm - almost like it was her duty as an American. That's when I knew she was the girl for me."

Nate Forrest, Tupelo, MS

Homemade Potato Chips

Full of natural potato flavor, these chips are the perfect accompaniment to cheeseburgers and sandwiches. The ⅛-inch thickness ensures a potato chip that is both hearty and crisp. You won't be able to eat just one, or five, or ten!

2 large baking potatoes,
    peeled and cut into ⅛-inch slices with a mandolin or sharp knife
peanut oil for frying
kosher salt
cracked black pepper

Fill a heavy pot with peanut oil to a depth of 3 inches and heat to 350 degrees. After slicing, pat the potato slices dry with a paper towel. Add the potatoes to the pot in 2-3 batches and fry until golden brown. Drain on paper towels and sprinkle with kosher salt and black pepper. Serve immediately or store in an airtight container.

Makes 4 servings

"The food in the South is as important as food anywhere because it defines a person's culture."

Fannie Flagg, actress, comedian and author

Roasted Corn Salad with Avocado

This wonderful salad tastes like summer in a bowl. It showcases some of the best ingredients of the season. Roasting the corn until it is dark and slightly charred brings out a deliciously sweet and smoky flavor.

Salad:

6 ears fresh corn, husks removed

olive oil for brushing

3 cups grape tomatoes, cut in halves

½ red onion, chopped

½ green pepper, chopped

1 medium avocado, peeled, pit removed,
   cut into small chunks

½ cup fresh cilantro, chopped

8 oz. feta cheese, crumbled

Preheat oven to 400 degrees. In a small mixing bowl, whisk together the vinaigrette ingredients. Set aside.

Brush the ears of corn with olive oil. Place them on a baking sheet and roast for 30-35 minutes until they begin to brown. (Hint: line the baking pan with aluminum foil for easy clean up).   Allow to cool. On a cutting board, remove the corn from the ears using a sharp knife.

In a large mixing bowl, combine corn and all remaining salad ingredients. Add the vinaigrette and toss to coat. Serve immediately or refrigerate.

Makes 8 servings

Vinaigrette

¾ cup olive oil

4 Tbsp. lime juice

2 tsp. ground cumin

1 ½ tsp. chili powder

½ tsp. salt

¼ tsp. black pepper

"We all eat, and it would be a sad waste of opportunity to eat badly."

Anna Thomas, author, screenwriter and producer

Meeting Street Peach Cobbler

½ cup (1 stick) butter

1 cup all-purpose flour

2 cups sugar, divided in half

1 Tbsp. baking powder

¼ tsp. salt

1 cup milk

4 cups fresh peaches, peeled and sliced (if fresh peaches are not in season, canned or
frozen may be substituted)

1 Tbsp. lemon juice

Preheat oven to 375 degrees.

Place the butter in a 13 x 9-inch baking dish and melt in the oven. Set aside. In a mixing bowl, combine the flour, 1 cup sugar, baking powder and salt. Add the milk and stir just until the dry ingredients are incorporated. Pour the batter over the melted butter in the pan but do not combine.

In a saucepan, combine 1 cup sugar, peaches and lemon juice. Stirring continuously, bring to a boil over medium-high heat. Pour the peach mixture evenly over the batter in the baking pan but do not combine. Bake for 45 minutes until golden and bubbly. Serve warm. May be topped with vanilla ice cream or whipped cream, if desired.

Makes 8 servings

Old Fashioned Sunday Supper

The Menu

Carolina Southern Fried Chicken

Summer Tomato Tartlets

Sweet & Crunchy Broccoli Salad

Cheddar Cheese Biscuits

"Cooking is at once child's play and adult joy.
And cooking done with care is an act of love."

Craig Claiborne, American author and journalist

"I almost wish we were butterflies and liv'd but three summer days - three such days
with you I could fill with more delight than fifty common years could ever contain."

John Keats (1795-1821) English poet. *Bright Star: Love Letters and Poems of John Keats to Fanny Brawne*

There is comfort in tradition, and food is no exception. Perhaps we are simply creatures of habit, but oh how dear we hold our time-honored customs and the recipes we associate with them. This is not to suggest that we don't have a flair for experimentation in the kitchen or love clipping and sharing new recipes. We do. My particular downfall is whipping up new creations then forgetting to write down how I made them. Having said that, we southerners also have a particular reverence for sharing our traditional dishes with loved ones. I call it "meaningful food." It comforts us body and soul. It is a joyous part of happy celebrations and a beautiful expression of love and condolence in sad moments when mere words will not suffice. The intertwining of family, friends, food and tradition is undeniable. I have found this to be especially noticeable when grown children return home and ask for special family dishes to be prepared. If you've ever doubted the association between food and nostalgia, try doing what I did one Thanksgiving. My insinuation that I might experiment with a fancy new stuffing recipe was met with immediate disapproval and protest. "Oh no, please don't, Mom. We want the one you always make – the simple one with cornbread, celery and onions." Such a simple request, yet so full of meaning.

Carolina Southern Fried Chicken

This classic comfort food recipe from South Carolina gets a little kick from Old Bay Seasoning, a delectable blend of herbs and spices gifted to the South by the great state of Maryland. This is my favorite recipe for fried chicken, which is perhaps the most quintessentially southern dish of all.

1 (2 ½-3 lb.) whole chicken, cut into pieces

3 eggs

½ cup water

2 cups all-purpose flour

3 Tbsp. Old Bay Seasoning

2 Tbsp. salt

2 tsp. black pepper

vegetable shortening

In a medium bowl, whisk together the eggs and water. In a separate bowl, combine the flour, Old Bay Seasoning, salt and pepper. Dip each piece of chicken into the egg wash and then into the flour mixture, turning to coat thoroughly. Set aside.

In a deep skillet or Dutch oven over high heat, melt vegetable shortening to a depth of 2 inches. Heat until hot but not smoking. A drop of water dropped into the oil should pop. Add chicken to the skillet in a single layer. Do not overcrowd. You will likely need to cook the chicken in batches. Reduce the heat to medium and cook until brown on both sides, using tongs to turn chicken to avoid burning. White meat will typically take 10-12 minutes per side, while dark meat will take a few minutes longer. Allow chicken to drain on paper towels before serving.

Makes 4-6 servings

"Well of course there will be fried chicken in heaven. It is, after all, heaven."

Beatrice Hamilton, Florence, SC

"Folks think it's old fashioned and untrue to say that the way to a man's heart is through his stomach but I take exception to that. I've charmed many an eligible bachelor with my tomato pie recipe and it hasn't failed me yet. You might say it's my secret weapon. Well, that and a dab of Chanel No. 5 behind my ears."

Summer Tomato Tartlets

These colorful little beauties are so flavorful I could eat them three times a day during the summer. They're perfect for breakfast with scrambled eggs or eaten room temperature for lunch (no fork needed) with a glass of sweet iced tea. I love them paired with a good old fashioned fried chicken dinner like this one. This recipe makes me wish summer lasted all year long.

3 large tomatoes, chopped to produce
    2 cups, and drained on paper towels
    to absorb the excess juices
1 tsp. salt
½ tsp. black pepper
½ tsp. garlic powder

¼ cup fresh basil, chopped
½ cup sharp cheddar cheese, shredded
½ cup Monterey Jack cheese, shredded
¼ cup finely chopped onion
½ cup mayonnaise
Two (9-inch) pie crusts

Preheat oven to 375 degrees. Roll out the pie crusts on a flat surface. Place a tartlet pan on the crust and cut a circle around it that is 1 inch wider than the diameter of the pan. Lay the circle into the pan and press gently to fit, fluting the edges. Pre-bake tartlets for 10 minutes.

Divide the tomatoes and layer them evenly among the 6 tartlet pans. Over the tomatoes, sprinkle the salt, pepper, garlic powder and basil. Set aside.

Reduce oven temperature to 350 degrees. In a mixing bowl, combine the cheeses, onion and mayonnaise. Spread the mixture evenly over the tomatoes. Bake for 25 minutes until golden and bubbly. Allow to rest for 10 minutes before serving.

Makes 6 servings

Sweet and Crunchy Broccoli Salad

What a delectable way to eat your veggies. This combination of flavors (sweet and savory) and textures (crunchy and tender) yields a popular summertime salad that is always a crowd pleaser.

1 large crown fresh broccoli, washed and cut into bite-size pieces

½ red onion, finely chopped

½ cup golden raisins

1 cup mayonnaise

4 Tbsp. cider vinegar

¼ cup sugar

8 slices bacon, cooked crisp and crumbled

½ cup sunflower seeds

In a mixing bowl, toss together the broccoli, onion and golden raisins. In a separate bowl, whisk together the mayonnaise, cider vinegar and sugar. Pour over the broccoli and toss to combine. Refrigerate until ready to serve, at least 1 hour. Just before serving, toss in the crumbled bacon and sunflower seeds.

Makes 6 servings

"Life without biscuits? It makes me
sad to think of such a thing."

Annabelle Lee, Savannah, GA

Cheddar Cheese Biscuits

It's difficult to improve a really good buttermilk biscuit, but adding a generous amount of sharp cheddar cheese is a great start. Warm and cheesy, these biscuits will be hard to resist. Remember to keep the buttermilk and butter cold to ensure a light, flaky biscuit.

4 cups all-purpose flour

½ tsp. baking soda

2 Tbsp. baking powder

2 tsp. salt

1 Tbsp. sugar

¾ cup (1 ½ sticks) cold butter

1 ½ cups buttermilk

1 cup plus 3 Tbsp. sharp cheddar cheese, grated

Preheat oven to 450 degrees. In a large mixing bowl, combine the flour, baking soda, baking powder, salt and sugar. Cut the cold butter into small chunks and, using a pastry cutter, two knives or a food processor, cut the butter into the flour mixture until it resembles coarse meal. Add the buttermilk and 1 cup of the cheese and mix just until combined. Do not overwork. Turn the dough out onto a well-floured surface. Gently pat the dough to a thickness of ½-inch. Cut out the biscuits using a round cutter (don't twist) and place them on a baking sheet so the edges are touching each other. Bake 9 minutes or until the biscuits are golden. Remove from the oven and sprinkle with the remaining 3 Tbsp. cheddar cheese. Serve warm.

Makes 12-14 servings

AUTUMN

"Come, little leaves," said the Wind one day;
"Come to the meadows with me and play.
Put on your dresses of red and gold;
For summer is past and the days grow cold."

George Cooper, American poet

Autumn Seafood Meal on the Patio

The Menu

Baked Brie with Fruit Chutney

Citrus Ginger Pan Seared Salmon

Fall Root Vegetable Gratin

Orange Salad with Sweet Sesame Dressing

Oatmeal Butterscotch Cookies

"The preparation of good food is merely another expression of art, one of the joys of civilized living."

Dione Lucas, English chef and first female graduate of Le Cordon Bleu

Gentler fall temperatures beckon us to dine outdoors in ways that most southerners cannot resist. It may have seemed that the hot mugginess of summer would linger forever, yet along comes the welcome and sweet relief of autumn. For me, it's never a moment too soon. The simplest things are what I appreciate most, like opening the windows at home and feeling a cool breeze cross through the house. How about the scent of burning leaves, the changing colors of the trees and the piles of pumpkins and gourds at every corner fruit stand? Yes, indeed, autumn is a true delight. However, it's not only the sights and scents I covet, but the abundance of rich and hearty autumn fare. Seasonal dishes such as spiced apples, baked acorn squash with cinnamon, sweet potato pies and pumpkin walnut bread are enough to make this a favorite season for us all! Our late afternoon seafood supper showcases some of fall's most delicious bounty. I set an old wrought iron table on the patio under a canopy of trees and covered it with a runner and table linens in warm earthy shades of amber, garnet and brown. An antique wooden bowl filled with apples and sprigs of boxwood plucked from the garden makes a naturally beautiful centerpiece.

"My nearly grown children have been teasing me lately that the older I get the more I talk about food - what I just ate, what I'm eating now, what I plan to eat later… that sort of thing. I neither deny this accusation nor make excuses for it. On the contrary, I consider it my obligation as a southern woman to pay my food the proper attention and forethought it deserves. I remind my children that once the foolishness of their youth has slipped away, they too will find the contemplation of 'what's for dinner' to be a favorite topic of discussion."

Cora Pate Mulford, Marietta, GA

Baked Brie with Fruit Chutney

1 (1 ½ lb.) wheel of Brie

1 sheet frozen puff pastry dough, thawed

¾ cup Fruit Chutney

1 Tbsp. butter, melted

Preheat oven to 425 degrees.

Slice off the top rind of the Brie and discard. Lay out the puff pastry dough on a greased baking sheet and place the round of Brie in the center. Spread ¾ cup chutney over the Brie and carefully fold the dough over the top, pressing to seal the edges. Brush the pastry with the melted butter and bake 20-25 minutes until the pastry is golden brown. Let cool for 10 minutes before serving.

Makes 8 servings

Fruit Chutney

½ cup water

½ cup sugar

1 cup dried fruit mix, chopped

½ tsp. salt

½ tsp. cinnamon

¼ tsp. ground nutmeg

In a medium saucepan, bring the water to a boil. Add the sugar and stir until dissolved. Reduce the heat. Add the dried fruit mix, salt, cinnamon and nutmeg. Cover and simmer for 30 minutes, stirring occasionally. Remove from the heat and cool to room temperature.

Citrus Ginger Pan Seared Salmon

1 tsp. ground ginger

1 ½ tsp. garlic powder

⅓ cup soy sauce

⅓ cup orange juice

¼ cup honey

4 - 6 salmon filets (approx. 6 oz. each), skin removed

3 Tbsp. olive oil

2 Tbsp. fresh dill, chopped

In a bowl, whisk together the first five ingredients. Transfer the marinade to a self-closing plastic bag. Add the salmon filets, seal the bag and turn to coat evenly. Refrigerate for 1-2 hours.

Heat the oil in a skillet over medium-high heat. Add the salmon filets and sear for about 7 minutes. Flip the filets and continue cooking for 5-7 minutes. Salmon is done when it is no longer translucent inside and flakes easily with a fork. Remove the filets to a serving platter and sprinkle with fresh dill.

Makes 4-6 servings

Fall Root Vegetable Gratin

1 ½ lbs. baby Yukon gold potatoes, cut into chunks

2 medium parsnips, peeled and cut into chunks

3 large carrots, peeled and cut into chunks

1 large red onion, coarsely chopped

6 Tbsp. olive oil, divided in half

2 cloves garlic, minced

¾ cup Panko bread crumbs

½ cup mozzarella cheese, shredded

½ cup Parmesan cheese, shredded

1 tsp. salt

Preheat oven to 450 degrees. Spread potatoes, parsnips, carrots and onion on a large baking sheet. Toss with 3 Tbsp. olive oil and the garlic. Roast for 30-40 minutes until vegetables are tender, slightly dark and caramelized. To ensure even roasting, toss the vegetables once or twice during the cooking time.

While the vegetables are roasting, combine 3 Tbsp. olive oil, bread crumbs, mozzarella, Parmesan and salt in a mixing bowl. Transfer the roasted vegetables from the baking sheet to a shallow baking pan and cover evenly with the bread crumb and cheese mixture. Return to the oven for 5-10 minutes, until the cheese is melted and the bread crumbs are toasted.

Makes 6 servings

Orange Salad with Sweet Sesame Dressing

The cool sweetness of this citrus salad makes it a perfect accompaniment to our warm autumn meal. It is best assembled right before serving. In lieu of fresh oranges, canned mandarin orange segments make a deliciously acceptable substitution. The dressing recipe makes more than needed, so store the extra in the refrigerator up to 3 weeks. It's wonderful on any salad.

4 cups orange segments (peeled, with toughest membranes and seeds removed)

1 (4 oz.) pkg. crumbled feta cheese

1 (3 oz.) pkg. sliced or slivered almonds

2 Tbsp. butter

1 tsp. salt

Melt the butter in a small bowl in the microwave. Toss with the almonds and spread evenly on a baking sheet. Place under the broiler in the oven and toast until golden brown, tossing once or twice for even browning. Watch carefully to avoid burning. Sprinkle with the salt. Set aside to cool.

Arrange the orange segments on a serving platter, shallow bowl, or individual salad plates. Sprinkle with the feta cheese and toasted almonds. Drizzle a generous amount of the Sweet Sesame Dressing over the salad and serve.

Makes 4 servings

"*Food is symbolic of love when words are inadequate.*"

Alan D. Wolfelt, American author and teacher

Sweet Sesame Dressing

⅓ cup cider vinegar

¾ cup sugar

1 tsp. dry mustard

1 tsp. onion powder

½ tsp. salt

½ tsp. paprika

1 cup vegetable oil

3 Tbsp. sesame seeds

Blend the vinegar and all dry ingredients except the sesame seeds in a blender until smooth. Gradually add the oil until fully incorporated. Transfer the dressing to a bowl, serving jar or storage container. Stir in the sesame seeds by hand. Shake or stir before serving.

Makes about 2 cups

"A balanced diet is a cookie in each hand."

Barbara Johnson, American author and comedian

Oatmeal Butterscotch Cookies

1 ¼ cups all-purpose flour

1 tsp. baking soda

½ tsp. cinnamon

½ tsp. salt

¾ cup butter, softened

¾ cup sugar

¾ cup brown sugar, packed

2 eggs

1 tsp. vanilla extract

3 cups rolled oats

1 ⅔ cup butterscotch chips

Preheat oven to 375 degrees. In a medium bowl, combine the flour, baking soda, cinnamon and salt.

In a separate large mixing bowl, beat the butter, sugar and brown sugar. Add the eggs, one at a time, and vanilla. Mix well. Gradually add the flour mixture, beating until smooth. Stir in the oats and butterscotch chips and combine well. Drop the dough by heaping tablespoonfuls onto a baking sheet. Bake for 8-10 minutes until golden brown.

Makes 2 dozen

Warm Hearthside Dinner on a Cool Evening

The Menu

Creamy Autumn Pumpkin Soup

Stuffed Pork Roast with Spinach and Feta

Herbed Baby Potatoes

Balsamic Roasted Brussels Sprouts

Spice Cake with Maple Buttercream Frosting

"As a child, there were very few words which I regarded with such welcome anticipation as 'Come to the table! Dinner's ready!'"

Jeannette Mulford, Charleston, SC

Hearty dinners and delectable autumn flavors are just two of many reasons to celebrate this season. Dining hearthside during cool weather is always a nice change of pace. I love adorning the table with all manner of seasonal décor and always abide by the belief that it doesn't have to be fussy or expensive to be beautiful. The look for tonight's dinner table was achieved ever so simply by purchasing a yard or two of burlap, cowhide, and faux leather from the fabric store and layering them all to create a warm effect. Allow yourself to be creative. Vary the heights of your centerpieces as I did with this stately pheasant which pays homage to the season and the pinecone candlesticks which elevate the candles so they cast a warm and welcoming glow over the table.

"The sights, scents and unquestionable beauty of autumn are gifts from above.

God must love us very much to bestow such a treasure."

Sarah Livingston, Beaufort, SC

"I have a theory about soup and its ability to sooth us body and soul. First of all, good soup is nothing short of creamy, liquid comfort in a bowl. I could eat it every day and often do, especially on the days when I'm feeling grumpier than usual. Secondly, soup forces us to slow down. Think of it. No one can successfully rush while eating soup. If you do you will spill it on your shirt. Eating soup is a deliberate act that requires a spoon and some degree of focus and calmness. It requires a more relaxed attitude than, say, gulping down a sandwich. I guess you could say that soup is the "elixir of tranquility". I may be overstating it a bit, but then again I'm biased when it comes to soup."

Beatrice Hamilton, Florence SC

Creamy Autumn Pumpkin Soup

2 Tbsp. olive oil

3 cups chopped yellow bell pepper (about 2 med.)

1 ½ cups chopped carrot (about 2 med.)

1 cup chopped onion (about 1 med.)

2 cloves garlic, minced

¾ tsp. smoked paprika

5 cups chicken broth, divided

1 (15 oz.) can pumpkin

3 tsp. salt

2 Tbsp. sugar

1 cup whipping cream

Heat oil in a Dutch oven over medium-high heat and sauté the yellow peppers, carrots and onions until soft and tender, about 20 minutes. Stir in the garlic, paprika and 2 cups chicken broth. Bring to a boil. Cover, reduce heat and simmer for 20 minutes. Transfer the vegetable mixture to a blender or food processor. Add the pumpkin and process until smooth. Return the mixture to the Dutch oven and add remaining 3 cups chicken broth, salt, sugar and whipping cream. Whisk until smooth and heat until piping hot. Ladle soup into individual bowls and garnish with large crispy croutons.

Makes 8-10 servings

Stuffed Pork Roast with Spinach and Feta

2 Tbsp. butter

½ medium onion, finely chopped

¾ cup chicken broth

½ tsp. dried sage

1 tsp. salt

2 cups cornbread dressing crumbs

½ cup golden raisins

3 cups fresh spinach, finely chopped

1 (4 oz.) carton crumbled feta cheese

3 lb. fresh pork roast

salt and pepper

Preheat oven to 350 degrees. In a large skillet, melt butter over medium-high heat. Add onions and sauté until soft, about 5 minutes. Remove from heat. Add chicken broth, sage and salt. Stir to combine. Add cornbread crumbs, raisins, spinach and feta cheese. Toss gently to combine. Set aside.

Double-butterfly the pork roast as follows: Starting in a corner, cut lengthwise, separating the top two-thirds from the rest of the roast (Figure 1) without cutting all the way through. Open this section onto the cutting board as if opening a book. Starting at the center line of the roast, repeat this process by cutting the two-thirds (left side) in half again (Figure 2) without cutting all the way through. Pound the roast, if necessary, to a thickness of about ½ inch. Generously salt and pepper both sides (Figure 3). Spread the stuffing mixture evenly on top of the roast, stopping ½ inch from all sides (Figure 4). Starting on one end, tightly roll up the roast (Figure 5). Using kitchen twine, securely tie the roast every two inches (Figure 6). Place the roast in a roasting pan and cook for 50-60 minutes, until the internal temperature reaches 130-135 degrees. Allow roast to rest for 10-15 minutes. Carve into 1 inch slices and serve with *Orange-Ginger Sauce*.

Makes 8 servings

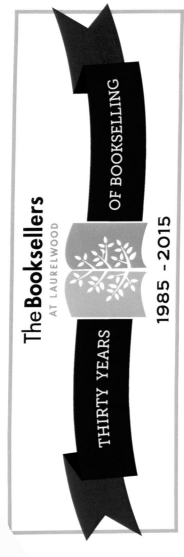

The**Booksellers**
AT LAURELWOOD

THIRTY YEARS OF BOOKSELLING

1985 - 2015

The **Booksellers**
AT LAURELWOOD

'85 '15

30 YEARS OF BOOKSELLING

Thank you,
Mid-South, for
letting us share
your love of
reading since
1985.

mon - thurs
7:30 am-9 pm
fri 7:30 am-10 pm
sat 8 am-10 pm
sun 9 am-8 pm

387 Perkins Road
Extended
Memphis, TN
38117
901-683-9801

Orange-Ginger Sauce

⅓ cup brown sugar, packed

2 Tbsp. cornstarch

2 cups orange juice

½ tsp. ground ginger

Combine the brown sugar and cornstarch in a saucepan. Add the orange juice and ground ginger. While stirring, bring to a boil over medium-high heat. Reduce temperature and simmer, stirring until slightly thickened, about 5-7 minutes.

Makes about 2 ½ cups

Herbed Baby Potatoes

2 lbs. small potatoes (Yukon Gold or new potatoes are nice.)

2 tsp. salt

4 Tbsp. butter, cut into chunks

2 Tbsp. flat leaf parsley, chopped

2 Tbsp. chives, chopped

salt and pepper

Place the potatoes in a large saucepan and add cold water to cover them completely. Add the salt and bring to a boil. Lower the heat and simmer until the potatoes are fork tender, about 7-9 minutes depending on size. Drain the potatoes, keeping them in the saucepan. Add the butter, parsley and chives and toss gently until butter is melted. Add salt and pepper to taste.

Makes 6 servings

Balsamic Roasted Brussels Sprouts

1 ½ lbs. Brussels sprouts, cut in half

3 Tbsp. olive oil

2 Tbsp. balsamic vinegar

2 Tbsp. brown sugar

salt and pepper

Preheat oven to 425 degrees. Trim the Brussels sprouts of any brown ends or yellow leaves. In a medium mixing bowl, toss them with the olive oil, balsamic vinegar and brown sugar. Spread the Brussels sprouts evenly on a baking sheet and roast for 25-35 minutes, tossing once or twice with a spatula for even browning. Remove from oven and sprinkle generously with salt and pepper.

Makes 6 servings

Maple Frosting

¼ cup (½ stick) butter, room temperature

½ tsp. salt

⅓ cup maple syrup

2 tsp. vanilla extract

3 cups powdered sugar

2 Tbsp. milk

In a mixing bowl, combine the butter, salt, maple syrup, vanilla and ½ of the powdered sugar. Alternating between the two, add the milk and the remaining powdered sugar. Mix until smooth.

Makes 2 cups

Spice Cake with Maple Buttercream Frosting

2 cups brown sugar, packed

1 stick butter, room temperature

½ cup vegetable oil

5 eggs, separated

2 cups all-purpose flour

1 tsp. baking soda

1 tsp. baking powder

1 tsp. cinnamon

2 tsp. ground ginger

½ tsp. nutmeg

¼ tsp. ground cloves

¼ tsp. salt

1 cup buttermilk

Preheat oven to 350 degrees. Grease and flour two round (9-inch) cake pans. Cream the brown sugar and butter in a large mixing bowl with an electric mixer. While mixing, add the oil in a steady stream. One at a time, add the egg yolks, beating well after each one.

In a separate mixing bowl, sift together the flour, baking soda, baking powder, cinnamon, ginger, nutmeg, cloves and salt. With the mixer running, begin adding the flour mixture and the buttermilk to the batter by alternating between the two until well mixed.

In a separate bowl, beat the egg whites with the electric mixer until stiff peaks form. Fold the egg whites into the batter. Pour the batter into the two prepared cake pans. Bake for 25 minutes or until a toothpick inserted in the center comes out clean. Cool on wire racks.

Invert the cake pans and carefully remove both layers. Place one layer on a serving plate. Spread a layer of Maple Frosting on the top of the bottom layer. Place the second cake layer on top. Spread the remaining frosting on the top and sides of the cake. Garnish with autumn leaves if desired.

Makes 16 servings

A Hearty Brisket Feast

The Menu

Chili-Beer Beef Brisket

Chopped Harvest Salad with Cherry Vinaigrette

Cheesy Scalloped Potatoes

Honey-Ginger Carrots

Sweet Potato Pie with Cinnamon Whipped Cream

"Dining partners, regardless of gender, social standing, or the years they've lived, should be chosen for their ability to eat — and drink — with the right mixture of abandon and restraint. They should enjoy food and look upon its preparation and degustation as one of the human arts."

Mary Frances Kennedy Fisher, American food writer

One of the keys to planning a delicious meal is to select dishes that offer a variety of flavors, textures, temperatures and colors. This autumn brisket dinner is a fine example. Our tangy brisket is definitely the star of the show, while the creamy, cheesy potatoes and tender, sweet carrots are great accompaniments. A harvest salad, with its crisp, cool sweetness and gorgeous colors rounds out the plate. Did you say dessert? Top it all off with a warm slice of old fashioned Sweet Potato Pie and you've got yourself one fabulous autumn meal.

Chili-Beer Beef Brisket

I doubt there's a simpler way to prepare a savory beef brisket than this recipe. Let the crock pot do its job while you take full credit for a deliciously moist and tender brisket. In the unlikely event that there are leftovers, may I suggest a brisket sandwich for lunch tomorrow?

2 ½ - 3 lb. beef brisket

1 medium onion, chopped

2 garlic cloves, minced

2 tsp. salt

1 tsp. black pepper

1 (12 oz.) jar chili sauce

1 (12 oz.) can beer

Place the brisket, fat side down, in a crock pot. Cover the brisket with the onion, garlic, salt and pepper. Pour the chili sauce over the brisket and cook on low setting for 5 ½ hours. Pour the beer over the brisket, raise the heat to high and cook for 1 hour. Remove the brisket from the crock pot to a cutting board and allow to rest for 10 minutes. Slice thinly and serve with remaining sauce.

Makes 8 servings

Chopped Harvest Salad with Cherry Vinaigrette

The seven ingredients below constitute seven reasons you will love this salad – eight if you count the fabulous cherry vinaigrette. Take liberties with this recipe and try out some of your own favorite additions like apples or pears. This salad also makes a great lunch dish by topping it with some chopped chicken or grilled salmon.

2 heads romaine lettuce, coarsely chopped

1 large cucumber, chopped

1 large vine ripe tomato, chopped

1 medium red onion, chopped

½ cup dried cherries

½ cup chopped walnuts

1 (4 oz.) pkg. crumbled blue cheese

In a large bowl, combine all ingredients and toss with Cherry Vinaigrette. Serve immediately.
Makes 4-6 servings

Cherry Vinaigrette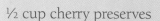

½ cup cherry preserves

¾ cup canola oil

¼ cup red wine vinegar

1 Tbsp. sugar

2 cloves garlic, minced

½ tsp. salt

In a bowl, whisk all ingredients until well blended. Store unused dressing in an airtight container.
Makes 1 ½ cups

"I'm going to break one of the rules of the trade here. I'm going to tell you some of the secrets of improvisation. Just remember — it's always a good idea to follow the directions exactly the first time you try a recipe. But from then on, you're on your own."

James Beard, American author, teacher, columnist and TV personality

"Home is the place I prefer to be. I have seen much of the world — traveled here and there — but I'm always happiest when I'm at home, baking something in my own little kitchen or puttering around the garden. I imagine lots of folks feel that way. We all need a place where we can relax and just be ourselves."

Hattie Montgomery, Waynesville, NC

Cheesy Scalloped Potatoes

This comforting potato dish can also be made with Gruyere or cheddar cheese. It's perfect with beef brisket, but also wonderful alongside baked ham, ribs or fried chicken.

3 Tbsp. butter

2 lbs. (about 4 medium) baking potatoes, peeled and sliced ⅛" thick

1 medium onion, finely chopped

2 ½ cups Swiss cheese, shredded

½ cup Parmesan cheese, grated

2 ½ cups half-and-half

salt and pepper

Preheat oven to 350 degrees. Butter a large baking dish with 1 ½ Tbsp. of the butter. Layer the ingredients in the dish in the following order:

1. ⅓ of the potatoes
2. Salt and pepper
3. Half the chopped onions, ½ cup Swiss cheese and a sprinkling of Parmesan cheese
4. ⅓ of the potatoes
5. Salt and pepper
6. The rest of the onions, ½ cup Swiss cheese and a sprinkling of Parmesan cheese
7. Remaining potatoes
8. Half-and-half
9. Dot with the remaining 1 ½ Tbsp. butter

Cover the baking dish with aluminum foil and bake for 1 hour. Remove the foil and sprinkle with the remaining Swiss and Parmesan cheese. Bake, uncovered, for an additional 30-40 minutes until the potatoes are tender and the liquid is mostly absorbed.

Makes 8-10 servings

Honey-Ginger Carrots

When it comes to fresh vegetables, a simple preparation is always best. In this case, simple and delicious go hand in hand.

1 lb. whole carrots, peeled and cut diagonally into 1" lengths

¼ cup (½ stick) butter

3 Tbsp. honey

½ tsp. ground ginger

1 Tbsp. lemon juice

1 Tbsp. flat leaf parsley, chopped

Add the carrots to a pot of boiling water and cook until fork tender but still firm, about 5-6 minutes. Remove from heat and drain.

In a large skillet over medium heat, melt the butter. Add the honey, ginger and lemon juice and stir to combine. Add the carrots and toss to coat. Cook until heated through. Sprinkle the carrots with the parsley and serve.

Makes 6 servings

Sweet potato, sweet potato, it's so true,
Sweet potato, sweet potato, I love you.
Cook you up and mash you up and put you in a pie,
I could eat you every day and that's no lie.

Poem of unknown origin as recited by Annabelle Lee, Florence, SC

Sweet Potato Pie
with Cinnamon Whipped Cream

"Autumn in a pie crust" is how I'd describe this pie. I often make two pies as one is never enough, especially since I want to be sure there is some left for "breakfast pie" with coffee the next morning.

2 ½ cups (about 1 lb.) mashed
   sweet potatoes

½ cup (1 stick) butter, softened

1 cup sugar

½ cup milk

2 eggs

½ tsp. ground nutmeg

½ tsp. cinnamon

1 tsp. vanilla extract

1 (9-inch) unbaked pie crust

Preheat oven to 350 degrees. In a large bowl, combine the mashed sweet potatoes and butter. Add the sugar, milk, eggs, nutmeg, cinnamon and vanilla. With an electric mixer, beat on medium-high speed until smooth. Pour the sweet potato filling into the pie crust. Bake for 50-60 minutes until a toothpick inserted in the center comes out clean. Serve with Cinnamon Whipped Cream.

Makes 8 servings

Cinnamon Whipped Cream

1 pint heavy whipping cream, chilled

¼ cup sugar

1 tsp. vanilla extract

1 tsp. cinnamon

Place all ingredients in a stand mixer with a whisk attachment and whip on medium-high speed for 2-3 minutes or until soft peaks form.

WINTER ✥

"Winter is the time for comfort, for good food and warmth, for the touch of a friendly hand and for a talk beside the fire. It is the time for home."

Edith Sitwell, English poet

"The gentle art of gastronomy is a friendly one. It hurdles the language barrier, makes friends among civilized people, and warms the heart."

Samuel V Chamberlain, American author, photographer and artist

Welcoming Comfort Food Supper

The Menu

Balsamic Glazed Pot Roast with Sun Dried Tomatoes

Easy Almond Rice

Roasted Asparagus with Lemon Zest

Cherry Gelatin Salad

Molasses Crinkle Cookies

Attitude is everything when it comes to success in the kitchen. Well, that and a really good chuck roast. A little wine doesn't hurt either. Most importantly, allow yourself a bit of freedom to experiment. Recipes are guides; at least that's how I've always viewed them. If you don't care for something, change it. If you've got a different idea, try it. You may – or may not – be pleased with the outcome, but you will be a better cook for having tried. Also, do not fear failure. Some of my best recipes have come about after a string of less than stellar results. Just never give up. Tonight's menu is practically no fail. I love pot roasts because they are the most forgiving of all the braised meats. You can experiment with them all day long and they will likely still be delicious. Their savory aroma will draw your guests to the table in a trance-like state. Pot roast has that kind of power.

"Invest in what's real. Clean as you go. Drink while you cook. Make it fun. It doesn't have to be complicated. It will be what it will be."

Gwyneth Paltrow, actress and author

Balsamic Glazed Pot Roast with Sun Dried Tomatoes

3 ½ - 4 lb. chuck roast

4 Tbsp. plus 2 Tbsp. oil

1-2 large onions, coarsely chopped

1 (8 oz.) package sliced baby mushrooms

1 (3 oz.) package sun dried tomatoes

2 Tbsp. flour

1 ½ cups beef broth or stock

⅓ cup balsamic vinegar

⅔ cup red wine

3 cloves garlic, minced

½ tsp. smoked paprika

2 tsp. salt

½ tsp. pepper

Preheat oven to 350 degrees. Cut the roast into 6-8 pieces. In a 5-7 qt. Dutch oven, heat 4 Tbsp. oil over medium-high heat. Add the meat in a single layer and brown for 3-4 minutes on each side (Figure 1). Meat may need to be browned in 2 batches. Remove the meat to a plate.

Add the remaining 2 Tbsp. oil, onions, mushrooms and sun dried tomatoes to the Dutch oven (Figure 2). Sauté until the onions are tender. Add the flour and stir (Figure 3). Add the beef stock (Figure 4) and deglaze the pan by scraping up any brown bits. Add the balsamic vinegar (Figure 5), red wine, garlic, smoked paprika (Figure 6), salt and pepper. Stir until ingredients are combined, then return the chuck roast pieces and juices to the Dutch oven.

Lay a piece of aluminum foil on top of the Dutch oven and carefully press down until it touches the entire surface of the pot roast (Figure 7). Tightly seal the edges of the foil, crimping them over the top of the Dutch oven. Put the lid on top (Figure 8) and cook for 2 hours.

Makes 8 servings

Easy Almond Rice

By toasting the almonds, you'll bring out a deeper flavor that enhances this or any recipe. The easiest way to toast nuts is in a dry skillet over medium heat, stirring often, until golden brown.

3 cups water

3 cups uncooked instant rice

2 Tbsp. butter

1 cup slivered almonds, toasted

1 tsp. salt

½ tsp. pepper

2 Tbsp. fresh parsley, chopped

In a large saucepan, bring the water, rice and butter to a boil over medium high heat. Remove from the heat. Cover and let stand for 5-7 minutes or until the water is completely absorbed. Stir in the almonds, salt and pepper. Transfer to a serving dish and sprinkle with the parsley.

Makes 8 servings

Cherry Gelatin Salad

Most southerners will admit they love a good gelatin salad. They were once the rage in the South and sat atop nearly every holiday table. As with so many things, they fell from favor for a time, but I sense a revival. When it comes to the art of balancing flavors, textures and temperatures, nothing rounds out a heavy meal like the cool, fruity sweetness of a good gelatin salad. This old fashioned cherry salad is superb with our pot roast menu. Prepare it with confidence and serve it with pride!

2 cups boiling water

1 (21 oz.) can cherry pie filling

1 (8 oz.) can crushed pineapple, undrained

2 (3 oz.) pkgs. cherry-flavored gelatin mix

In a large mixing bowl, combine the bowling water with the next three ingredients until the gelatin is completely dissolved. Transfer the mixture to a serving dish. Refrigerate until set, at least 2 hours.

Makes 8 servings

"She felt about her zester the way some women do about a pair of spiky red shoes - a frivolous splurge, good only for parties, but oh so lovely."

Erica Bauermeister, author, *The School of Essential Ingredients*

Roasted Asparagus with Lemon Zest

This quick and simple recipe is my favorite way to prepare asparagus. For another variation, you could omit the lemon zest and splash the spears with balsamic vinegar.

1 bunch asparagus spears, ends trimmed

3 Tbsp. olive oil

1 tsp. kosher salt

½ tsp. black pepper

1 Tbsp. lemon zest

Preheat oven to 425 degrees. Place the asparagus on a baking sheet and drizzle with olive oil. Toss to distribute the oil evenly. Arrange the spears in a single layer. Sprinkle with salt and pepper. Roast in the oven for 13-15 minutes, until tender and slightly charred around the edges. Sprinkle asparagus with lemon zest. Serve immediately.

Makes 4 servings

Molasses Crinkle Cookies

Molasses is the dark brown, syrupy by-product of sugarcane when it is refined into sugar. Its deep sweetness, combined with ginger, cinnamon, nutmeg and cloves, gives these cookies a wonderfully rich and spicy flavor.

¾ cup butter, room temperature

1 cup sugar

1 large egg

¼ cup molasses

2 cups all-purpose flour

1 tsp. baking powder

1 tsp. baking soda

¼ tsp. salt

1 tsp. ground ginger

1 tsp. cinnamon

½ tsp. nutmeg

¼ tsp. ground cloves

Preheat oven to 375 degrees. In a large mixing bowl, beat the butter and sugar with an electric mixer until creamy. Add the egg and molasses and beat well until combined.

In a separate bowl, combine the remaining ingredients. Add the flour mixture, a cup at a time, to the butter and sugar mixture, using the electric mixer to beat well after each addition. Chill the dough in the refrigerator for 30 minutes.

Drop the dough by heaping tablespoons onto an ungreased baking sheet. Bake for 10-11 minutes. Cool on a rack.

Makes 2 dozen

"Here in the South we like to cook for others and often give gifts of food to family and friends. These gifts send messages and different foods say different things. For example, when I give a casserole to a friend, I'm sending a wish of comfort and nourishment. However, when I give homemade cookies, I'm sending heartfelt cheer and happiness. After all, it's difficult to be unhappy when eating a cookie."

Hattie Montgomery, Waynesville, NC

A Cozy Winter Meal

The Menu

Shrimp Newberg on Biscuits

Whipped Sweet Potatoes with Candied Pecans

Poached Pears with Feta and Golden Raisins

Old Fashioned Buttermilk Pie

"Everyone should host a dinner party now and then. It's such a rewarding act of hospitality. I suggest keeping it simple. If the cake falls or you accidentally overcook the chicken, try not to fret. Just remember, most kitchen mishaps can be overcome by a good bottle or two of wine."

Virginia Beaumont, Thibadeaux, LA

"The fact is, I love to feed other people. I love their pleasure, their comfort, their delight in being cared for. Cooking gives me the means to make other people feel better, which in a very simple equation makes me feel better. I believe that food can be a profound means of communication, allowing me to express myself in a way that seems much deeper and more sincere than words."

Anne Patchett, American author and bookseller

Even if the weather outside is cold and gloomy, you can perk things up inside by creating a cheery setting for a wintertime dinner. Give your table a new personality by showcasing some cooler winter shades of blue, gray and creamy white. Our candlelit dinner table tonight layers a crisp off white tablecloth with blue patterned linens and vintage eyelet napkins. The decoratively carved white chargers (a bargain store find) set off the vivid blue dinner plates beautifully. It's always a good idea to have something from nature on the table, especially in the middle of winter when beautiful blooms are scarce. Try a variety of evergreen clippings from the yard as I did here. I placed sprigs of magnolia leaves, spruce and English ivy into a burlap covered vase for a fresh look.

Shrimp Newberg on Biscuits

Refrigerated or frozen biscuits may be used in this recipe, or opt for the homemade variety. My favorite biscuit recipe on p. 101 would work perfectly, just omit the cheddar cheese.

4 Tbsp. butter	½ tsp. salt
3 cups small or salad shrimp, cooked	½ tsp. cayenne pepper
¼ cup sherry	1 tsp. paprika
1 cup heavy cream	6 biscuits, split in half
8 egg yolks	2 Tbsp. chopped chives

Melt butter in a skillet or Dutch oven over medium heat. Add the shrimp and sherry and heat through.

Place the heavy cream in a medium saucepan. Whisk the eggs into the cream. Heat the mixture over medium heat until thickened, 8-10 minutes. Mix in the salt and spices. Add the cream mixture to the shrimp and heat through. When ready to serve, spoon the shrimp mixture over the split biscuits and sprinkle with the chopped chives.

Makes 6 servings

Whipped Sweet Potatoes with Candied Pecans

Although a potato masher will always get the job done when it comes to mashing white or sweet potatoes, an immersion blender makes especially quick work of this task. I love this tool since, like a hand mixer, it enables me to whip potatoes into submission with very little effort.

4 large sweet potatoes, peeled and cut into chunks

2 Tbsp. butter

2 Tbsp. brown sugar

¼ cup orange juice

Place the sweet potatoes in a large saucepan, cover with water and bring to boil over medium-high heat. Cook the potatoes until they are fork tender, about 12-15 minutes. Drain the potatoes, keeping them in the saucepan. Either mash the potatoes with a potato masher or whip them with an immersion blender or hand mixer until smooth. Add the butter, brown sugar and orange juice and mix well. Heat the potatoes through over medium heat. Transfer to a serving bowl and top with Candied Pecans.

Makes 8 servings

Candied Pecans

½ cup pecan halves

1 Tbsp. butter

1 Tbsp. brown sugar

Place pecans in a dry skillet over medium-high heat. Pan fry the pecans, stirring frequently, until pecans are slightly toasted, about 2-3 minutes. Reduce heat to medium and add the butter and brown sugar. Continue cooking for 3-4 minutes, stirring so that neither the butter nor the brown sugar burns. Pour the pecans out onto a sheet of aluminum foil and allow to cool.

Makes ½ cup

Oven Poached Pears with Feta and Golden Raisins

The warm, cinnamon-y fragrance of this dish as it bakes will make the house smell wonderful. It's also a great accompaniment to ham or roasted pork.

4 ripe but firm pears, peeled, cored and cut in half

⅓ cup sugar

⅓ cup brown sugar

¾ tsp. cinnamon

⅓ cup golden raisins

⅓ cup water

⅓ cup crumbled feta cheese

Preheat oven to 350 degrees. Trim the backs of the pear halves so they lay flat. Arrange the pears in a baking dish. Combine the sugar, brown sugar and cinnamon in a mixing bowl. Stir in the golden raisins. Fill the pear cavities with half the sugar mixture. Add the water to the remaining sugar mixture and pour around the pears.

Bake the pears until golden and tender and the sauce is syrupy, about 45 minutes. It may be necessary to add more water to the pan during the cooking time if the sauce becomes too thick. Add water, ¼ cup at a time, if needed. Arrange the pears on a serving platter and spoon the extra syrup on top. Sprinkle with the feta cheese and serve.

Makes 8 servings

"I never learned to cook. Now that I am retired and spending more time at home, I suspect I am becoming a bit of a nuisance to my wife in the kitchen. I have offered to help her and she has obliged by giving me a series of menial tasks like organizing the cupboards or taking out the trash. I was hoping for more responsibility. Finally last night she relented and taught me how to separate eggs for a hollandaise sauce she was preparing. I'm proud to say I did not break a single yolk. It made her smile. I think this bodes well for our future in the kitchen."

Nate Forrest, Tupelo, MS

Old Fashioned Buttermilk Pie

This classic recipe is pure old fashioned goodness. Top it with any seasonal fruit you enjoy. Berries are my favorite.

3 eggs

½ cup butter, softened

1 ½ cups sugar

3 Tbsp. all-purpose flour

1 cup buttermilk

1 ½ tsp. vanilla extract

2 Tbsp. lemon juice

1 (9-inch) unbaked pie crust

assorted fresh berries

Preheat oven to 350 degrees. In a medium mixing bowl, beat the eggs. Add the butter, sugar and flour and beat until smooth. Add the buttermilk, vanilla extract and lemon juice. Mix well. Pour the mixture into the pie crust. Bake for 45-55 minutes, until golden brown and the center is firm. Cool on a wire rack. Serve with fresh berries.

Makes 8 servings

"We must have pie. Stress cannot exist in the presence of pie."

David Mamet, American playwright

"One kind word can warm three winter months."
Japanese proverb

A Homestyle Family Dinner

The Menu

Classic Poppy Seed Chicken Casserole

Skillet Cinnamon Apples

Roasted Broccoli

Pumpkin Bread Pudding with Rum Sauce

Even if the weather outside is frightful, this table is so delightful you won't mind a bit. Tonight our table will be laid heavy with an array of winter comfort foods including a most beloved southern casserole, Poppy Seed Chicken. The cinnamon goodness of the skillet apples makes a perfect side dish and will fill the house with a spicy aroma. As I do with nearly all my vegetables these days, I roasted the broccoli to give it a dark and earthy flavor befitting this meal. The grand finale of tonight's show is a warm pumpkin bread pudding drizzled with rum sauce. It is a cousin to the peach bread pudding in my first book. This incarnation with pumpkin, pecans and rum sauce is a heavenly winter dessert.

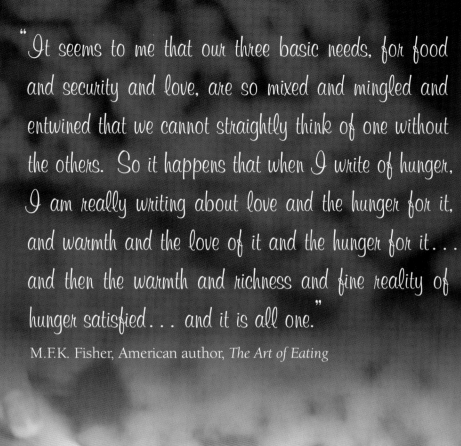

"It seems to me that our three basic needs, for food and security and love, are so mixed and mingled and entwined that we cannot straightly think of one without the others. So it happens that when I write of hunger, I am really writing about love and the hunger for it, and warmth and the love of it and the hunger for it... and then the warmth and richness and fine reality of hunger satisfied... and it is all one."

M.F.K. Fisher, American author, *The Art of Eating*

"I guess they call it comfort food because it makes you feel better. Like when I'm sick or I had a bad day and my mom makes macaroni and cheese and I feel better. It's like that."

James Edward Bearden, "Jeb", age 8, Montgomery, AL

Classic Poppy Seed Chicken Casserole

This popular southern dish is always a crowd pleaser. Warm and creamy, it defines comfort food in the South. Since it is so simple to prepare, try making an extra one or two to freeze for those busy weekday nights.

4 cups chopped, cooked chicken

1 (10 ¾ oz.) can cream of chicken soup

1 (16 oz.) container sour cream

1 Tbsp. poppy seeds

1 sleeve butter-flavored crackers, crushed

¼ cup butter, melted

Preheat oven to 350 degrees. In a large mixing bowl, combine the chicken, soup, sour cream and poppy seeds. Spoon the chicken mixture into a greased 2-quart baking dish. In a small bowl, combine the crushed crackers and melted butter; sprinkle the topping evenly over the casserole. Bake for 35-40 minutes, until hot and bubbly.

Makes 6 servings

Skillet Cinnamon Apples

This is a nice recipe to have on hand for many different dishes. It can be enjoyed as a side dish with just about any meal, spooned over pancakes, wrapped in pastry dough and baked, or topped with ice cream.

¼ cup butter

8 apples, cored and chopped

½ cup brown sugar

¼ tsp. ground cinnamon

¼ tsp. nutmeg

Melt the butter in a large, heavy skillet over medium heat. Add the apples, brown sugar, cinnamon and nutmeg. Sauté the mixture until the apples are golden and tender, about 15 minutes.

Makes 6 servings

"I know the look of an apple that is roasting and sizzling on the hearth on a winter's evening, and I know the comfort that comes of eating it hot, along with some sugar and a drench of cream. I know how the nuts taken in conjunction with winter apples, cider, and doughnuts, make old people's tales and old jokes sound fresh and crisp and enchanting."

Mark Twain, American author and humorist

Roasted Broccoli

The edges of the broccoli will become slightly charred as it cooks, resulting in a wonderful roasted flavor.

1 large bunch of broccoli (about ½ pound), washed and thoroughly dried

2-3 tablespoons olive oil

salt and pepper to taste

Preheat oven to 425 degrees. Cut the broccoli into medium-size pieces and place in a bowl. Drizzle with olive oil and toss to coat thoroughly. Spread the broccoli evenly onto a baking sheet. Sprinkle generously with salt and pepper. Bake 10 minutes; turn the pieces over and then bake an additional 10 minutes.

Makes 4 servings

Pumpkin Bread Pudding with Rum Sauce

1 large loaf challah or French bread,
  cut into cubes (approx. 10 cups)

2 cups heavy cream

2 cups milk

5 eggs

1 ½ cups sugar

1 ½ tsp. cinnamon

1 (15 oz.) can pumpkin

½ cup chopped pecans

Preheat oven to 350 degrees. In a large bowl, whisk together the cream, milk, eggs, sugar, cinnamon and pumpkin.   Add the bread cubes and toss gently to coat. Let sit for 15 minutes.

Lightly coat a 10 x 14-inch baking pan with butter or cooking spray. Pour the bread and egg mixture into the pan and press gently. Sprinkle the pecans evenly over the top. Bake 50-60 minutes or until a toothpick inserted in the center comes out clean. Serve warm or room temperature with Rum Sauce.

Makes 12 servings

Rum Sauce

½ cup (1 stick) butter

½ cup heavy whipping cream

1 ½ Tbsp. rum or 1 tsp. rum extract

1 cup sugar

Combine all ingredients in a saucepan over medium heat. Cook and stir until mixture is smooth and sugar is dissolved. Do not boil.

Makes about 2 cups

"I admit that sometimes I eat my dessert at the beginning of the meal. Why should I wait until the end and run the risk of being too full to enjoy it? Eating dessert whenever you choose is one benefit of being a grown up."

Beatrice Hamilton, Florence, SC

"First we'll make snow angels for two hours, then we'll go ice skating, then we'll eat a whole roll of Toll House cookie dough as fast as we can, and then we'll snuggle."

Buddy the Elf

Recipe Index

Kitchen Techniques & Table Tips

✦❦ Thank you, Earl. ❦✦

My deepest gratitude goes to my fiancé and white knight, Earl Ehrhart, for his unfailing love. Earl, your encouragement and belief in me has carried me through this book writing process and sustained me through life's journey in more ways than I can count. This book, as well as my own happiness, would not be possible without you. I am so thankful for the privilege of becoming your wife.

"Forever thine, forever mine, forever ours."

✦❦ More heartfelt thanks to... ❦✦

My best friend, Pam Sanders, who lets me just be myself (this means she lets me ramble on and on) and still loves me anyway. Every girl needs a best friend and I hit the jackpot. Pam, from our early days together in church youth choir (occasionally skipping to go to Dairy Queen) through the ups and downs of our busy adult lives, you have been a constant and loving presence. You are the epitome of a steel magnolia and I admire you for a thousand different reasons. Thank you for being everything that a best friend should be.

"I love you more than my luggage!"

Jarrod Cecil, my truly gifted photographer with a can-do attitude and an impeccable eye for culinary beauty. Thanks to you, my book is more than a compilation of recipes and stories; it is a visual work of art.

My sweet friend and business associate, Pam Short, for her dedication and hard work assisting with the production of *Seasons in the South* and our other exciting business ventures. Your constant encouragement has been God's blessing to me.

Lynn Taylor, my dear friend, business consultant, advice-giver and all-around great woman. You've been with me for the long haul and how I appreciate your Godly wisdom, invaluable advice and unfailing friendship.

Brian Mayfield and the great folks at Techquidation, Inc. who take my book to the world! We've come a long way from the days when I had 5,000 books in my garage. Thank you for all your hard work, professionalism and great business advice.

Judy Sparks and Katie Cash of Smartegies, LLC, for their creative vision and invaluable professional direction. Thanks also to Aveline Hayes for the beautiful design and layout of this book. It's not easy for a control freak like me to hand over the creative process to someone else, but I couldn't have been in better hands. You did me proud.

The thousands of wonderful gift and boutique stores across the country that have carried my first book, *Sunday in the South*, and will be selling this book too. What a love I have for these small businesses and their entrepreneurial spirit. After being on the road so much for the past several years and doing hundreds of book signings, I have seen firsthand the dedication, creativity and tireless work ethic of these American small business owners. I am so proud that my books have found an exclusive home in these beautiful stores.